THE
CRITICAL
LIFE SKILL

(Things You Need
to Overcome Life
Challenges)

By
Stephen
Ezeagu

ISBN:
978-978-988-939-6

The Contents

DEDICATION

This book is dedicated to God Almighty

who made it
possible for me to
come up with this
wonderful book.

ACKNOWLEDGMENT

I am indebted to my wife, Chizzy Beauty, and my son Saviour

for their
wonderful prayers
and support at all
times.

I also want to acknowledge you reading my book right now.

There's no "**The Critical Life Skills**" without you. Thanks a million.

Chapter One

Chapter Three

Knowing the
Importance of
Your Zero Limits

Chapter Four
Get Rid of Fear

Chapter Five

Chapter Six

Chapter Seven

Chapter Eight

Chapter Fifteen

The back book heading

YOUTHFUL AGE IS THE TRANSITION FROM CHILDHOOD WITH HIDDEN TREASURES TO THE UNKNOWN FUTURE WITH GREAT AND MIGHTY OPPORTUNITIES, FILLED WITH UNSEEN AND UNDREAMED REALITIES FOR FULFILLED ADULTHOOD

To overcome Life
challenges you
need critical life
skills.

Challenges in life are inevitable so long you live. You can only overcome them with wisdom and other forms of life skills. Some challenges in life only come to make you strong and more responsible.

People who are overcome by life challenges are people who confront the situation the way it comes to them without applying any of the skills.

Any challenge that comes to you at a particular time has its way of tackling the situation. Some situations require violence while some peaceful confrontation.

Any attempt to use one in place of another will cause damage.

Something happened in my working place. To the extent that, it wanted to cost me my salary for the whole of that month.

The issue even generated a lot of controversies that are unprecedented in the company.

What happened: Either cashiers,

inventory, or
somebody else
made a mistake on
a particular item
on my goods shelf,
because there I
work as a sales rep.
It is a
supermarket.
Then, the

assistant auditor, by the name Alaba, blamed me. This man from the beginning has been working against many staff in that company to gain favor from the owner of the company.

Every staff of the company saw what happened, and they said it is not my fault and That why must the man be that wicked.

From the

beginning, one of my supervisors has been siding him because he pretends very well, which many staff could attest to it.

Thank God for God-fearing

people in the
company who
stood by me till
justice prevailed.
In the end, I
survived and
prevailed.

What do you
think would have
happened if I

did not use
wisdom to follow
up on the matter?
Of course, it could
have resulted in
another thing
entirely.

Either good or
bad.

Until I Come
Your Way Again.

...keep in touch!

Made in the USA
Las Vegas, NV
11 January 2023

65405274R00022